YOU AND YOUR GRANDCHILDREN

YOU AND YOUR GRANDCHILDREN

Special Ways to Keep in Touch

Sunie Levin
Illustrations by Margie King

PRICE STERN SLOAN
Los Angeles

To our grandchildren
Amanda, Danny, David, Jillian, Megan, Rachel and Sean

Copyright © 1991 by Sunie Levin

Published by Price Stern Sloan, Inc.
Los Angeles, California

Printed in United States of America.

10 9 8 7 6 5 4 3 2 1

This book is printed on acid-free paper.

ISBN: 0-8431-2873-9

Library of Congress Cataloging-in-Publication Data

Levin, Sunie.
   You and your grandchildren / by Sunie Levin.
      p. cm.
   Includes bibliographical references.
   ISBN 0-8431-2873-9
      1. Grandparenting—United States.   2. Grandparent and child—United States.   I. Title
HQ759.9.L48 1991
306.874'5—dc20   90-25803
                                                                          CIP

God could not be everywhere so he created parents
And when they became too busy he created grandparents. . .

TABLE OF CONTENTS

HOW YOU CAN BUILD MEMORIES WITH GRANDCHILDREN OF ALL AGES

APPENDIX A
CHILDREN'S BOOKS ABOUT GRANDPARENTS

APPENDIX B
GRANDPARENTING BOOKS

INTRODUCTION

As soon as my first daughter got married, I could hardly wait to become a grandmother. No kidding. But it was a different story for my husband. He hated the idea. With a passion. He used to growl at his three girls, "I'll disown the first one of you who makes me a grandfather." He refused to let anyone call him a senior citizen, and would not take advantage of that special little card that gives you a discount at the movies.

That was until Jillian was born. As soon as he saw that heart-shaped little face, it was love at first sight. You still can't call him a senior citizen, but he sure doesn't mind being called Grandpa! The same thing occurred six more times—a total of seven grandkids, all equally precious. But all not equally accessible. Three lived in town, and we could see them as often as we wished and enjoy each first tooth and first day at school. But four lived more than a thousand miles away, and we got to see them twice a year if we were lucky. What frustration. We didn't want to be strangers to them.

What to do? Well, that's what this book is all about. We had to use every possible strategy, as well as invent some new ones, to stay in touch. A lot of them came naturally; some took imagination.

I have to admit that at times the good old days—when Grandma sat in her rocking chair and all the grandchildren came over to her house everyday— looked easy. The grandparents' home served as a refuge from the day-to-day discipline kids received from their parents. Grandparents had time to listen and make the grandchild feel special. And they were close by.

Today, as often as not, if you want to see the grandchildren, you're talking two boarding passes each way, missed connections, lost luggage and airline food—how many bags of peanuts can you eat? Yet it's well worth it. But the problem is, how can you keep the little ones from forgetting you between visits? It can be done, and I'm going to tell you how to do it. Many of the ideas in this book are ones that have worked for me or that were shared at grandparenting workshops by grandparents who didn't want their grandkids to forget them between visits.

How your infant grandchild
can learn
to recognize you

BABY, YOU FEEL SO GOOD!

You lucky grandparent: You've been asked to help out with your newborn grandchild. So put some tape on your mouth in case you forget and try to give advice. Here's a chance to get bonded early. Holding, cuddling, touching, kissing—in other words, concentrated affection—is the key. Babies love to be stroked and petted, and their soft skin is wonderful to touch. Feel them snuggle up into your shoulder. Is there anything in life that feels that good? Grandpa's strong arms make an infant feel especially secure.

Be sure and talk all the time you are touching your grandchild. Don't give a newborn a bottlefeeding, bath or change of diaper without talking. "Hey, you beautiful baby, do I have some great food for you" or "Grandpa's going to give the most gorgeous baby in the world a wonderful bath." Sing songs. Make noises while you stroke your grandchild—you'll both love it. Rhythmic humming while you're holding and walking the baby is great—the resonance from your chest vibrates directly against the infant and gives him* an enormous sense of security.

*The pronouns "he" and "him" are used instead of "he or she" and "him or her" for the sake of simplicity.

I SEE GRANDMA AND GRANDPA

It is rare for a child less than one year old to remember you when there are a number of months that elapse between visits. But it's startling to have the child scream in terror at the sight of your face when you get off the plane. Okay, so you didn't freshen up your makeup, but does he have to act as if you just stepped out of the Friday night fright show?

It doesn't have to happen. Here is a suggestion on how to promote bonding and easy recognition of you between visits. Send an enlarged photograph (at least 16'' by 20'') to be hung on the wall near the infant's crib. This will help him know you when you come to visit.

One grandmother told me that she sent her one-year-old grandson an 8'' by 10'' picture that was hung next to his high chair so he could point to the picture and talk to it when he eats. At this early age I can't guarantee that the child still won't scream when he sees you, but at least he should quiet down sooner.

I HEAR GRANDMA AND GRANDPA

During the first few months of your grandchild's life, send a ten-to-fifteen minute tape recording of your voice. Now, carrying on a one-sided conversation with a month-old baby might seem a little strange, but grandparents naturally get a little crazy over their latest grandchild, so nobody is going to think you're a candidate for the funny farm. Begin by saying, "Hello (child's name)" and at the end "Good-bye (child's name)." During the tape, say the child's name and whatever name you would like to be called several times. Speak slowly and leave time for the child to listen. Sing or hum a tune, a soothing lullaby or a rub-a-dub bath song. It doesn't matter if you don't sing well, your grandchild won't be critical.

After three months sing playtime songs such as pat-a-cake. It will give you and your grandchild much pleasure. When you visit your grandchild, begin to sing these songs and he will associate them with the ones he has heard daily. This will help him feel comfortable with you because you'll be a familiar part of the nursery scene. Parents should play the tape frequently so that your voice will be easily recognized. When you call on the telephone and speak to your grandchild, he will know you.

GRANDMA AND GRANDPA SMELL GOOD

I bet you can close your eyes and remember the aromas of your own grandparents' house. All those yummy cooking smells, Grandma's lotion, Grandpa's pipe and those wonderful sweet lilac bushes.

Along with sights and sounds, an infant responds to smells. If Grandma wears a special perfume or powder and Grandpa an after-shave lotion, douse some on sachet or cotton balls tied into a pretty cloth ball. Send these scents to be hung near your picture. When your grandchild sees you in person, there will be a familiar smell that will help associate you with your picture.

How you can build
a good relationship with
your growing grandchild

READ ME A BEDTIME STORY

Children are usually interested in books long before it occurs to parents to begin reading to them. If you have the chance to be with your grandchild at bedtime, there's no sweeter moment. This is an opportunity to cuddle up close with a favorite book—the tenderness seems to bubble of its own volition. And there are so many wonderful picture books to help your grandchild develop a love for reading (see Appendix A).

If you live across town or are a long-distance grandparent, you can call your grandchild on the telephone and read a special story. Be sure the child also has the book so he can follow along. For times when you aren't able to call, make a cassette tape with several bedtime stories that you know he likes.

LET'S EAT WITH GRANDMA'S RED-AND-WHITE DISH

Mealtime is special and can have a lot of happy associations. Wouldn't it be nice to know that your grandchild thinks of you three times a day? Give him a set of personalized dishes. There are companies that will reproduce your picture on their cups and plates. You can add "Love and kisses" and your name. For an infant you could get a terrycloth bib with "Grandma's Little Angel" or "Grandpa's Little Champ" printed on it. As the infant becomes a toddler, a personalized play apron with an attached hand towel is great for sticky fingers. The important message is don't forget Grandma and Grandpa!

GRANDMA AND GRANDPA SENT ME MY SECURITY BLANKET

There is a special blanket, a magic blanket, that never leaves a child's side for the first few years of his life. It is soft and snuggly and smells a special way and gives oh-so-much comfort at nap time and bedtime. It is one of the most important possessions in your grandchild's life and will be carried around for many years to come. You should only be as important to the child as that blanket! It goes with him everywhere to help dry up all the tears and fears. If it is ever lost, the house is turned upside down until it is found.

Send two receiving blankets, one with Grandma's and one with Grandpa's name, just in case one is temporarily lost. And if the child becomes more attached to the one that doesn't have your name on it, well, whoever said life was fair? Although you would love to cuddle, stroke and kiss your grandchild, it might not be possible if you are too far away. But wouldn't it be nice to know that you are constantly with your grandchild even though it's only through his magical blanket.

BATH TIME WITH GRANDPA'S
LITTLE YELLOW DUCKY

Bath time is usually the highlight of the day. It deserves a special yellow ducky from Grandpa and perhaps a green frog from Grandma. A tape of your singing rub-a-dub would be a big hit. Or you could send a tape of bath-time songs recorded by a popular children's entertainer.

ONE-SIDED CONVERSATIONS

As soon as your grandchild begins to talk, it is important for you to talk to him each time you call your children. Be sure to send a play telephone for practice before the real calls begin. When you call, say your grandchild's name and the name the child calls you several times. Sing a song, recite a short poem, and when you ask a question supply the answer. Although there may be little or no response on the other end except for a few sounds, your grandchild is listening. Keep calling on a regular basis so that your voice becomes familiar to your grandchild.

One of these days the most exciting words you will ever hear is when he says "Grandma" or "Grandpa" or whatever name he might call you. Isn't it amazing the names we think are cute just because the grandchild thought them up? I know one grandma who is called "Buggy Bee." I know another one called "Witchy." Send a picture of yourself talking on the telephone—it can be held up to the child when you call to help build mental associations.

PICTURES ARE ALMOST LIKE BEING THERE

Keep sending pictures as often as possible, especially a few from old family albums that include your own children with you. I bet you never guessed when you saved those old snapshots how handy they'd become. They help your grandchild identify you as part of the family group. Also send recent pictures of you with your grandchild so as he learns to recognize himself he will see you. Include a few action pictures of things you are doing in and around the house: raking leaves, working in the garden, walking the dog or baking cookies.

When you cannot be together for special holidays or birthdays, send a videotape. If you don't have a video camera try to borrow or rent one. For the younger child read a bedtime story or sing a familiar song. For the older child tell a riddle or joke and include some of the plans you have for your next visit. Even if the riddle is ridiculous and the joke is rotten, children are indulgent. They're a great audience—they think everything is funny.

I DREAM OF GRANDMA AND GRANDPA

Bedtime is a special time, and it would be nice for your grandchild to think about you before he falls to sleep. Make a cassette of several short bedtime stories and a few poems that can be listened to each night. Sometimes Mommy and Daddy have had a hard day and are too busy for a bedtime story, but Grandma and Grandpa are never too busy. This would also be a good time for your grandchild to look at pictures of you before going to sleep. One grandparent had a photograph imprinted on a pillow slip so that her five-year-old Amanda could kiss the grandparent's pillow goodnight after saying her prayers.

MAKE-BELIEVE TIME

For the young child, playing make-believe is an enchanting time when the imagination can soar into the future. Children love to play "When I grow up, I want to be. . . ."

Make-believe time can be shared with a grandparent in person, on the telephone or in letters. Imaginary friends and role-playing can bring about peals of laughter and hours of fun. Don't forget to provide a box of old clothes, hats and a wig or two for when they come to your house. Let's be honest about this: You're getting as big a kick out of it as they are! And you should be! It's the greatest thing in the world, provided you participate with them. Just giving them a box of grown-up things won't do it. You need to be active!

How you can keep in touch with your school-age grandchild

LET'S PLAY A GAME

Watch your grandchild's eyes light up as you say, "Let's play a game!" The child loves the challenge and competition and most of all your attention. Carry a deck of cards in your pocket and you'll be ready for a game of Slap Jack, Go Fish or Spades. With a pad of paper and a pencil, you can play Ticktacktoe, Hangman or unscramble some words. Think back to some of your own favorites. Your grandchild will get right into Chinese Checkers, Marbles or Dominoes. Playing these games will help him develop the ability to follow directions and solve problems, which will be important in school.

It's easy to let your grandchild win and see his big smile, but it's important that the child learn how to lose. No one really likes to lose, but it's a part of life. Tell your grandchild when he doesn't win that it's good to play with someone who is better than himself because he will learn from that person. A judicious mixture of letting the child win sometimes and lose others is probably the best. If he always wins he'll sense early on that the games are fixed, and then winning loses all of its satisfaction. Be sure and discuss fair play and cheating. And when the inevitable day comes when your grandchild starts beating you fair and square, be a good sport about it!

TELEPHONES BUILD BRIDGES
ACROSS THE MILES

As your grandchildren grow, the telephone can be an important tool to help you become close to them. If your calls are frequent you can exchange ideas, help with problems, play games, swap jokes, plan visits and generally become a part of their daily lives. They'll be excited and waiting for your call if you learn their daily schedule and phone when you know you won't be interrupting anything. Grandchildren will often listen to grandparents' advice because they don't hear it on a daily basis. It is important to let them know they are missed and that you think they are great.

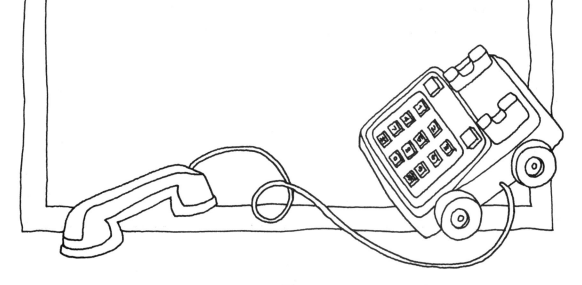

THE RIGHT GIFT MAKES A BIG DIFFERENCE

Parents can't always afford to buy all the wonderful things their children would like, but grandparents like to indulge their grandchildren. The grandchild says "I want" and the grandparent responds "Let's go see if we can find it." Although the parent might appreciate clothing, children prefer a book, tape, toy or game. Don't send young children money; it doesn't leave a lasting impression or remind them of you. Older children, however, do enjoy shopping for a gift with money that you've sent them.

If your grandchild is going to be celebrating a birthday or special holiday, send him your package a couple weeks early; it will be more meaningful if it isn't opened with a number of other presents. Your grandchildren respond to the attention you give in sending something just for them.

GUESS WHAT? GRANDMA AND GRANDPA
SENT ME A CAKE!

How proud the youngster is when he announces to friends at his birthday party, "Grandma and Grandpa sent me a Big Bird cake." When you cannot be at the party, send a cake to remind your grandchild that you would like to have been there and are thinking about him. If you can bake the cake yourself and figure out how to send it so it will arrive in one piece, fine. If your cakes are the kind that could break toes if they were dropped, arrange for a bakery to have one delivered. As grandchildren get older you can send a bouquet of flowers or balloons. Mylar balloons are great; some kids keep them in their rooms for months.

I GOT A LETTER IN THE MAIL

Children find it very exciting to receive mail addressed to them. The letter you write should be on stationery that is easily recognized as yours. For example, your grandchild can quickly learn that the letter is from you when it comes in a specially colored envelope. For toddlers, cut out pictures from a magazine to tell a story. Their parents can add a few words when they read the story.

For grandchildren six years and older, start a grandletter program. This means that you would write stories about your life and send them to your grandchildren to keep in a scrapbook. You would then keep a journal of your thoughts about each correspondence, and this would act as a record of you to be appreciated by your grandchild when he is an adult. By frequently exchanging letters, postcards and cassette tapes, you and your grandchild can build a firm and lasting relationship despite the distance that separates you.

FAMILY NEWSLETTER

Sending a family newsletter to your grandchildren is a great way to have them know you and help establish family closeness. You can send it as often as you like. Be sure and save a copy for your grandchildren's scrapbook. Share any happy events that occur during the year. Headlines that read SEAN WINS TROPHY IN SOCCER! or JILLIAN JUMPS OFF HIGH-DIVING BOARD! are sure to win your grandchildren's approval and add to their self-esteem. After all, they take after you, so you know the kind of egos they have. Don't forget to include things about yourself such as GRANDPA GROWS TWO-POUND TOMATO! or GRANDMA WINS TENNIS MATCH! The family, especially your grandchildren, will love seeing their names in print.

One column can be entitled "I remember when. . . ." There can be contests and a collection of jokes. All family members should contribute, including great-aunts and -uncles. While the main purpose of the newsletter is to communicate with the grandchildren, it becomes a wonderful tool for the entire family to share.

PARCEL-POST GRANDPARENTS

Children love surprises, and they become so excited when they receive a colorfully wrapped present in the mail. Parcel-post packages remind your grandchildren that you are thinking of them. And it's important to send things not just for special occasions, but throughout the year. It's not how expensive the gift is that matters—it's the thrill of being surprised and remembered.

WHEN YOUR GRANDCHILD IS ILL

When your grandchild has an illness that is going to last at least a week or require hospitalization, he will appreciate and need attention. Cards, small gifts and letters will show him that you care. Send him a card each day so that he always has something to open. You might include treats, stickers, notes, small trinkets and I.O.U.s for future activities. Puzzles, games and books make the time go by and let your grandchild know that you would like to be with him. I can guarantee that your attention will be enjoyed. A few words of encouragement on the telephone as well as a reminder from you that the illness won't last forever also will lift his spirits.

YOUNG SCHOOL-AGE CHILDREN

As your grandchildren grow older, your telephone conversations and letters can include discussions about their favorite T.V. shows, hometown baseball or football teams or about their pets. There are many participation gifts that you both can enjoy. Books about magic tricks, riddles, crossword puzzles and jokes can become a secret adventure that only grandparents share with their grandchildren. If they are old enough, encourage them to read the directions and do the magic tricks for their friends. The next time you call, you can check on what the reaction was to the tricks. If you both have computers you might be able to exchange computer data via modem. Or try working a crossword puzzle at the same time over the telephone (this can be time-consuming and, therefore, expensive if you're calling long-distance). Any of these activities provide lots of fun for both grandparents and grandchildren.

OLDER SCHOOL-AGE CHILDREN

Your grandchildren in the upper elementary grades might enjoy writing you letters in secret code. They are also entertained by puzzles, ventriloquism, juggling, puppetry, hobby kits, crafts and photograhy. In addition, you could exchange recipes, make tapes and put together scrapbooks or picture albums. Buying a telescope and sharing astronomy is another experience most children love. But if you don't think a telescope is practical, try a pair of binoculars. And don't forget the story of your life and what happened in the good old days. If great-grandparents are still alive, have them tape their recollections. This can be an invaluable way to maintain memories and will be a continued source of wonder for the child.

COLLECTIONS MAKE MEMORIES

Collections that you start when your grandchildren are small can grow with them and give you a shared interest. If the collectibles are easily broken or expensive, keep them at your house until your grandchild is older. Keep in mind, however, that the collection belongs to your grandchildren. Both girls and boys enjoy animals, stamps, seashells, coins, records, cards and miniatures. Many collections can be passed down from generation to generation.

FAMILY SCRAPBOOK AND PHOTO ALBUM

An important link to each family's history is the scrapbook and photo album. When a prospective bride or groom is about to join a family, this is one of the first exposures they have to the family members. (Usually they go ahead with the wedding anyway.) Your grandchildren will enjoy having their very own scrapbook and photo album. Begin the album with pictures of their own parents as children. Include a few of you when you were younger (it lets the grandkids realize that you were the same age as their parents and gives them a sense of history and change). Of course, they never really believe that you were once that young, but at least they'll find the pictures amusing.

Remember to add photos of them as infants, especially if you are also pictured. Shots of family vacations and special holidays are great to include. Ask your grandchild to help you write the captions for the pictures. Also include letters and cards that were written and any news articles that appeared about the family members. When you feel the grandchild is old enough, give him the scrapbook to maintain.

How you can build memories with grandchildren of all ages

PLANNING A FAMILY REUNION

Oh no, not that again! The last family reunion ended with your doing all the work and listening to all the relatives complain. Aunt Tillie didn't speak to anyone, two sisters were openly hostile and all the grandchildren were clamoring for attention at once. Who needs all that hassle? But without these family gatherings for major holidays, where would the memories be of all the rituals unique to each family?

The so-called era of the disappearing family can be brought back with the family reunion. Being "home for the holidays" does give children and adults a profound sense of connection. Grandchildren anticipate these occasions with great delight. And adults, if truth be told, feel sad if the ritual holiday reunion is skipped. So what can be done to make it more fun for the adults? Plan it away from home at a central meeting ground so no one is burdened with all the work. Rent several RV's and meet at a campground or national park. Half the fun is in the planning. Write letters! Solicit ideas so everyone can play a part. Plan contests, give prizes and most of all, have fun. Even the fiascos will be laughingly recalled.

HOW YOU CAN KNOW
YOUR GRANDCHILDREN

To establish a good relationship, it is important for you to know your grandchildren. Do you know their interests, their favorite toys, the T.V. programs they enjoy or if they have a hobby? It is important to know your grandchildren's schedules: when they leave for school, when they return and their after-school activities. When you know your grandchildren then you'll have a lot to talk about on the telephone or in your letters. You can discuss their soccer-game scores or whether they have mastered a tumbling feat. You have to really care about these things and learn enough detail so that they know you're genuinely interested. Ask them to send you pictures of any sporting event that they participate in. It makes them feel important—and who among us doesn't want to feel important?

HOMETOWN NEWS

One of the best ways to keep up with what is going on in the town where your grandchildren live is to subscribe to the Sunday edition of their local newspaper or at least buy one periodically. You'll have a lot of local news to discuss with your grandchild when you call. You'll know everything from what is happening with the hometown team to special shows that your grandchild might want to attend. You might like to arrange for tickets for the child and a friend or take the grandchild yourself if you are coming to town. If you see an interesting article you can discuss it in the next call. Jokes or cartoons can be shared, a crossword puzzle can be worked jointly and your grandchild might read you the funnies. Knowing the local news will help your grandchild realize that you are interested in what is going on and that you want to be a part of the hometown scene.

SPORTS FANS

If your grandchildren enjoy sports, this is a terrific way to get closer to them. Learn about the sport that turns them on, whether it's baseball, football, soccer, gymnastics, swimming, horseback riding—whatever. This is something that kids really get excited about. When you care too, you become just that much more important to them. If possible, take them to games whenever you get the chance. If they belong to Little Leagues, become knowledgeable about the position they play. During the National Playoffs for baseball and football, encourage them to try and guess who is going to win. You might even have a small wager with your grandchild. You get the idea. Sports and grandparents are a natural, and you'll learn a lot too.

WHEN YOU VISIT
YOUR GRANDCHILDREN

You're missing your grandchildren so it's time for a weekend visit. Try not to disrupt their routine too much; sometimes it's better for you to stay at an inexpensive motel rather than stay at their house. If more than two grandchildren are in the household, I can almost guarantee this is a better arrangement. If it is summertime, a visit to a swimming pool or a zoo will be a hit with the younger crowd. Bring a tomato plant or two to plant with your grandchildren. They can report to you how many tomatoes they are able to harvest. Teaching your grandchild how to fly a kite or build a model airplane is also a wonderful experience for both of you.

Again, it can't be emphasized too strongly how important it is to take each grandchild somewhere individually. An hour of one-on-one attention is worth more than a whole week of a tumultuous family get-together in which the commotion cancels out any getting-to-know-you possibilities.

WHEN YOUR GRANDCHILDREN VISIT YOU

This is a golden opportunity to build strong bonds. Take advantage of it. Plan for it so you don't waste precious time. Research in advance the facilities your community has to offer that are in easy driving distance and that would appeal to kids.

Take them without their parents. This gives you a great chance to know them better, and they you. The parents will appreciate it too! For the young child, visiting the park or baking cookies will provide mutual fun. For the older child, putting up a bird feeder and identifying birds could be interesting. Write a limerick together: You write the first verse, have your grandchild write the second and take turns writing verses until it is finished. The important aspect of all these activities is the time that you give to them.

NO ONE COOKS LIKE GRANDMA

The restaurant may be posh and the food divine, but in your memory no one can cook as good as Grandma! Many families build their entire holiday celebration around Grandma's kitchen. Christmas Danish cookies, sweet-and-sour red cabbage and tomatoes stuffed with Italian salad may be some of her prize recipes. Potato latkes and matzo ball soup for Chanukah can be as much a part of the family celebration as lighting the Chanukah candles.

Most of the time, recipes aren't written down but passed on by word-of-mouth from mother to daughter. When you begin thinking of the pecan pie that Grandma used to make your mouth starts watering. Many grandchildren reminisce that "everything tasted better at Grandma's"—than anyplace else in the world.

If you can't be there for the holiday, perhaps you can send one of your favorite foods. It will guarantee that at least for a few minutes during the meal you will be thought of and remembered.

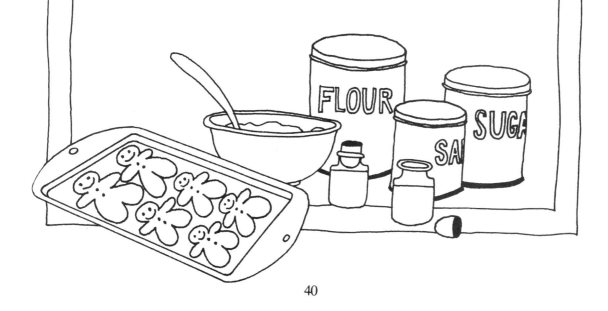

TAKING GRANDCHILDREN ON VACATION

The old adage about seeing life through the eyes of a child holds special meaning when it is your grandchild. If you really want to get to know your grandson or granddaughter, take him or her on a short trip. You'll not only get to know the youngster, you'll get to know whatever's going on in the family. Children tell everything they know. Don't act shocked if the child announces, "Mom and Dad took a shower together last night!" And if there is more than one child in the family, take only one at a time. This eliminates the bickering and sibling rivalry. More important, you have the chance to give the child all of your attention.

Planning the trip with your grandchild can be almost as much fun as the trip itself. For the young child, staying at a motel with a swimming pool can be an exciting weekend. With children older than eight, a fishing, camping or hiking trip in a national park will evoke pleasant memories for years to come. The American Youth Hostel memberships are reasonable and offer lodging in picturesque settings that include docked ships, mountain lodges, castles and converted hotels. Most of all, this vacation affords you the chance to really get to know your grandchild.

MORE THAN ONE GRANDCHILD

When you have more than one grandchild, you need to spend equal time with each one. If you visit them or they come to see you, plan an afternoon or even an hour with one at a time. They are totally different kids when they aren't with their parents or siblings—they're always better! You make them feel important because you want to be with only them. Plan something that you know they will enjoy. It might be reading a favorite book, playing a game or lunching at a special restaurant. The activity isn't as important as the attention you will give them.

SPOILING AND DISCIPLINING YOUR GRANDCHILDREN

As a grandparent you feel you have earned the right to spoil your grandchildren. And you have! That's what grandparents are for. Your own children seem to expect it, and the grandchildren love it. You don't see them very often, and it's hard for you to say no because you want them to like you. Usually they will want to please you and will take discipline better from you than from their own parents. If they're in a situation in which they could hurt themselves or if they are exceeding your limits, you have to be firm or try to negotiate a compromise. They have to know that at some point you can say no and mean it. You may be surprised, but they won't hold it against you.

If the parents have been extremely permissive in bringing up the children, you will have a problem. Let the parents and the grandchildren know up-front that at your house you set the rules.

WHEN THEY CONFIDE IN YOU

Being a long-distance grandparent makes it a little more difficult to be a confidant, but sometimes it can happen. Grandchildren frequently tell grandparents secrets that they won't tell their own parents. They will often listen to grandparents' advice because they feel the grandparents are less apt to nag or criticize. Treasure their trust in you and don't give away their confidence. It can be very tempting to tell their parents the cute things they told you. Don't pass along the fears and concerns they have expressed. If you feel it is important that you share some of the information with the parents, do so in a way that doesn't damage the trust that they have placed in you. Most things aren't important enough to risk letting the child down. If you develop an open communication with your grandchild, as he grows older you may be able to help and guide him with more serious problems.

"HELP! I CAN'T READ"

All young children look forward to the time when they are able to read for themselves. But some very intelligent children are unable to learn to read at grade level. Unfortunately, parents can rarely tutor their own children. It's amazing how we can be patient with everyone in the world but our own kids. You remember! With grandparents, however, it's different. A child will often accept suggestions from a grandparent. If your grandchild is having difficulty in the primary grades, send him books with accompanying tapes. It would be even better if you made the tape so he could hear your voice and words of encouragement. Speak slowly and tell the child when he should turn a page. You might have the weekly spelling list mailed to you so you can ask your grandchild to spell the words over the telephone.

Your grandchild, however, may be so upset by difficult work and constant failures that he will stop trying. When this happens it will be quite important for you to offer suggestions and alternate ways he might learn. If your older grandchild is several years below grade level, have duplicate social studies and science textbooks sent to you so you can tape each chapter. The most important thing you can do is to let your grandchild know that he will improve and that you think he is great.

CREATING A FAMILY HEIRLOOM

A baby quilt, shawl or christening gown that's lovingly made by hand is sure to be cherished for generations. An afghan, embroidered tablecloth or patchwork bedspread takes many hours of time, but time well-spent when you know it can be enjoyed for years to come. How wonderful to be able to say it was made by Great-great-grandmother. Granddad doesn't have to be an expert at woodworking to make a toy chest filled with wooden toys for the grandchildren to play with when they come to visit. One grandfather's project was to build a scaled-down dollhouse that was a replica of the grandparents' real home. He is also building a wooden castle that's sure to be a hit with his grandchildren.

These special projects demonstrate in a most concrete manner the caring that you truly feel, and each item becomes more meaningful as the years go by.

FAMILY RITUALS

Rituals and shared experiences bind family members together. As your grandchildren grow older, the rituals and traditions will become part of their heritage. Like an old family recipe, a fondness for certain customs is often passed down through the generations. Childhood rituals can contribute to the child's feeling of security and stability. And though later on he may make faces and tell put-down jokes about the obligatory family occasion, if it's omitted he'll miss it and feel a genuine void. Thanksgiving and other holidays at grandparents' house can become a tradition. As the child becomes an adult, singing the special songs and enjoying family foods will become cherished and wonderful memories.

Do everything you can to build this continuity. It is these predictable, ritualistic occasions that build the child's sense of family. Children like these annual events, although they may seem more like a tumult than a pleasure at the time. Don't underestimate their importance. Many young parents find themselves reenacting rituals with their children that are linked to happy memories of their own childhood.

THE GOOD OLD DAYS

It's difficult to know who enjoys stories about the good old days the most, the grandparents telling or the grandchildren listening. Children especially enjoy hearing about pranks that Mom and Dad played at their age. They like to hear war stories or what you did when you lived with Great-Grandpa. The war stories get more wonderful and heroic each year—try to make certain that they never learn that Grandpa's army days were spent as a clerk-typist in Fort Chaffee! Songs and family jokes are wonderful to share. Don't forget to bring out the old picture albums; the grandkids love them. These are the memories that can be passed down from generation to generation.

Make a tape recording of your reminiscences. Even better, if the great-grandparents are living, have them make one too. It will be a treasured family heirloom in years to come, and if any of your grandkids become interested in genealogy at some later date, your knowledge of the family tree will be invaluable. Much priceless information about the "old country" dies with the great-grandparents. Capture it now if you can.

And a final thought . . .

GRANDPARENTS ARE SPECIAL

Grandparents are never too busy to:

listen
tell stories
pretend
tell their grandchildren that they're great
make their grandchildren feel great
tell them what it was like in the good old days
be their friend

because they listen to their grandchildren not only with their ears but also with their hearts.

The attachment between grandparents and grandchildren is unique. Grandparents have the power to enrich their grandchildren's lives. Now that you've established an identity through telephone calls, photographs and letters, you and your grandchildren are not strangers when you see one another. By sending constant reminders, the relationship between you and your grandchild can be nurtured and strengthened even when you live far away from each other. It takes a little effort, but it is loving effort more than repaid by having a grandchild relate to you as a grandparent, not as a stranger.

APPENDIX A
CHILDREN'S BOOKS
ABOUT GRANDPARENTS

This guide is meant to help you select fine works of fiction and fantasy about grandparents and their relationships with their grandchildren.

ANNIE AND THE OLD ONE
by Miska Miles
A little Indian girl recognizes that her grandmother is going to die and learns to accept the cycle of life and death. The story is told with much caring. Ages 3-7. Little, Brown & Co.

CLOUDY WITH A CHANCE OF MEATBALLS
by Judith Barrett
Grandpa says that in the magical land of Chewandswallow meals come from the sky. But what happens when the weather changes? Ages 4-9. MacMillan Publishing Co.

DAWN
by Uri Shulevitz
The text of this lovely picture book comes from a Chinese poem about an old man and his grandson. They are asleep by the shore of a mountain lake, and dawn approaches. The full-color illustrations capture the subtle changes of light in the early morning. Ages 3-5. Farrar, Straus & Giroux.

FIRST FLIGHT
by David McPhaid
A young boy is going on his first airplane trip to visit his grandma. At the airport and in flight the boy calmly and carefully follows all the rules. One of his fellow passengers, a great big bear, finds the trip more difficult with hilarious results. Ages 3-8. Little Brown & Co.

GRANDADDY'S PLACE
by Helen Griffith
Janette doesn't like Grandaddy's place or the animals on the farm until she goes fishing with her grandpa. She changes her mind about everything and ends up having a wonderful time. Ages 5-9. Greenwillow Books.

GRANDFATHER TWILIGHT
by Barbara Berger
Day ends and Grandfather Twilight brings the miracle of night. Lovely illustrations and simple text present a poetic and reassuring picture as shadows deepen and the sun goes to rest. Ages 2-5. Putnam Publishing Group.

GRANDMA DRIVES A MOTOR BED
by Diane Hamm
Josh and his grandmother share happy times although her illness confines her to a motor-driven bed. Ages 4-8. Albert Whitman & Co.

GRANDMA GETS GRUMPY

by Emily A. McCully

Did Grandma really get grumpy? She loves kids and never complains about behavior or says "Stop!" like parents do. But things go too far when four cousins stay over night and act up. There are limits to even Grandma's patience. Ages 3-8. Ticknor and Fields.

GRANDMA IS SOMEBODY SPECIAL

by Susan Goldman

When you spend the night at Grandma's, it is always a wonderful experience because there is so much to do and she is there to do it with you. Grandma shares pictures of the child's parents and talks about the family. Ages 3-7. Albert Whitman & Co.

THE GRANDMA MIX-UP

by Emily Arnold McCully

Pip's mom and dad are taking a trip. Mom asks Grandma Nan to baby-sit. Dad asks Grandma Sal. The grandmas decide that they'll both stay and take care of Pip. But they can't agree on anything. Strict Grandma Nana likes a neat room; fun-loving Grandma Sal likes watching the ballgame on TV and sending out for pizza. Pip is used to doing things Pip's way. A fun book showing how a grandchild has to learn to deal with all types of grandparents. Ages 4-9. Harper & Row.

GRANDMA WITHOUT ME

by Judith Vigna

A young boy finds a way to keep in touch with his grandparents despite his parents' divorce. Age 3 and up. Albert Whitman & Co.

GRANNY IS A DARLING

by Kady Denton

Billy shares his room with Granny when she comes to visit. Although there are strange noises and scary things that happen, Billy protects Granny and learns not to mind the dark himself. A tender, funny, loving book just right for young children. Ages 3-7. Macmillan Publishing Co.

HOW OLD IS OLD?

by Ann Combs

Alistair, age four, is not quite sure how old "old" really is. His grandfather shows him, in charming rhyme, that old is a relative concept—that the answer to how old is old depends on who or what you are! Ages 4-8. Price Stern Sloan.

I UNPACKED MY GRANDMOTHER'S TRUNK

by Susan Hoguet

An alphabet adventure of twenty-six wonderfully improbable objects from an acrobat to a zebra all in irresistible rhyme. An excellent car game. Ages 3-8. Penguin U.S.A.

THE NAPPING HOUSE

by Audrey Wood

A snoring granny, a dreaming child, a dozing dog. This book is full of fun and surprises. The full-color illustrations make it a treasure. Ages 3-6. Harcourt Brace Jovanovich.

NIGHT JOURNEY
by Kathryn Lasky
Grandma Sashie visits with ten-year-old Rachel and tells her about her family's escape from Russia. Moving and well-written. Ages 10-14. Penguin U.S.A.

SEA SWAN
by Catherine Stock
After her grandchildren's visit, Grandma Elizabeth is restless and decides to learn something new. She buys an emerald green swimsuit and starts swimming lessons. A wonderful story about independence and self-respect that the young reader will recognize and share. Ages 6-10. Macmillan Publishing Co.

STINA
by Lena Anderson
Every summer when Stina visited her grandfather, she collected the treasures that the sea delivered. There were feathers, sea glass, smooth sticks—wonderful things. But nothing was as wonderful or as useful as the present that the huge storm sent. A warm, satisfying story of an adventurous and imaginative child and her understanding and imaginative grandfather. Ages 3-8. Greenwillow Books.

THROUGH GRANDPA'S EYES
by Patricia MacLachlan
A boy learns a rich and detailed way of seeing the world from his blind grandfather. Ages 4-9. Harper & Row.

THE TRAIN TO GRANDMA'S
by Ivan Gantschev
There's excitement and fun as grandchildren go to visit their grandparents on a fast steam train. Die-cut pages flip as the train plunges in and out of tunnels and over high bridges to where Grandma and Grandpa live. Ages 3-6. Picture Book Studio.

THE TROUBLE WITH GRANDAD
by Babette Cole
Grandad gets in trouble with the police when his tomato plant grows bigger than the police station and everyone thinks he may have a dangerous vegetable. Ages 3-6. Putnam Publishing Group.

THE TWO OF THEM
by Aliki
This is a quiet story about a grandfather who loved his granddaughter from the time she was born, and how when he died, she was able to remember things he had made for her and time they had spent together. A touching story. Ages 4-9. William Morrow & Co.

APPENDIX B
GRANDPARENTING BOOKS

The following is a list of books about grandparenting. There are only a few books written for and about grandparents. They include:

Cherlin, Andrew J. and Furstenberg, Frank. *New American Grandparent: A Place in the Family, a Life Apart.* Basic Books, 1986.

Elkind, David. *Grandparenting: Understanding Today's Children.* Scott, Foresman & Company, 1989.

Kornhaber, Arthur, M.D., and Woodward, Kenneth L. *Grandparents–Grandchildren: The Vital Connection*, Transaction Publishers, 1984.

Kornhaber, Arthur, M.D. *Between Parents & Grandparents.* Berkley Publishing Group, 1987.

LeShan, Eda. *Grandparents: A Special Kind of Love.* Macmillan, 1984.

McBride, Mary. *Grandma Knows Best But No One Ever Listens.* Meadowbrook Press, 1987.

Wassermann, Selma. *The Long-Distance Grandmother.* Rodale Press, 1988.

Wyse, Lois. *Funny You Don't Look Like a Grandmother.* Crown Publishers, 1988.

ABOUT THE AUTHOR

Sunie Levin, a noted educator with a Master's Degree in remedial reading and learning disabilities, was director of a learning-disability clinic in Kansas City, Missouri, for twenty years. She has taught university classes and has conducted training programs, workshops and seminars. Many of her remedial programs have been used throughout the country.

For the past several years she has been developing materials that strengthen the communication skills between grandparents and grandchildren. She also has been conducting grandparenting workshops and constructing methods to improve the relations between grandparents and grandchildren who are separated by distance. In her seminars—which she calls the "New Breed of Grandparents"—she helps find ways to desensitize problem situations and improve intergenerational relations.

Three of Sunie's grandchildren live in Kansas City; however, the other four live a considerable distance away, and she has felt the frustration of missing out on many of their first big events.